This book is about

....

....

My
Grandchildren
Memories of their Childhood

WRITING YOUR BOOK

Grandparenthood is one of the great joys of later years. The special connection between grandparents and grandchildren is usually a source of much happiness for everyone.

It is very natural to want to record the growth and progress of one's grandchildren. Because few of us are born to be authors, this book has been developed to make it easy and enjoyable for you to compile your own record of your grandchildren's early years.

Its simple structure and prompts will help you cover not only the major landmarks in their lives but also your more general thoughts on being a grandparent. There are sections about the times you have looked after

them or had them to stay, family events you have shared, schooldays and other aspects of their lives. There are even spaces for a few photographs and other mementoes, and a page on which to make a few notes about any holidays you have spent together.

You may wish to compile a different copy for each of your grandchildren, but the book has been designed to allow for the inclusion of two children in one volume.

In due course, what you write will become a valued family heirloom and a delight to future generations. Imagine the fun your grandchildren's children will have, reading what you have written!

CONTENTS

THE BIRTH 4

NAMING 7

THE EARLY YEARS 9

TAKING CARE OF THEM 13

COMING TO STAY 16

FAVOURITE THINGS 18

HOBBIES AND ADVENTURES 21

CHRISTMAS 24

BIRTHDAYS 27

OTHER CELEBRATIONS 29

HOLIDAYS 32

PRIMARY SCHOOL 36

SECONDARY SCHOOL 38

OVER THE YEARS... 40

THE FUTURE... 44

REFLECTIONS 46

THE
BIRTH

NAME OF GRANDCHILD

....

Born on ....

at ....

Weight at birth ....

Eye colour ....

Hair colour ....

Other distinguishing features ....

....

....

Do you remember your first

impressions? ....

....

....

....

....

....

....

....

....

....

....

....

FIRST
PHOTOGRAPH

A Mother with her Baby
CARLTON ALFRED SMITH (1853–1946)

THE
BIRTH

NAME OF GRANDCHILD

BORN ON

AT

WEIGHT AT BIRTH

EYE COLOUR

HAIR COLOUR

OTHER DISTINGUISHING FEATURES

DO YOU REMEMBER YOUR FIRST

IMPRESSIONS?

FIRST
PHOTOGRAPH

NAMING

GRANDCHILD'S FULL NAME

WHY WERE THESE NAMES CHOSEN?

WHO ELSE WAS THERE?

WAS THERE A CHRISTENING OR NAMING
CEREMONY AND PARTY?

DID YOU TAKE A GIFT?

WHO WERE THE GODPARENTS?

PHOTOGRAPH

NAMING

GRANDCHILD'S FULL NAME

WHY WERE THESE NAMES CHOSEN?

WHO ELSE WAS THERE?

WAS THERE A CHRISTENING OR NAMING CEREMONY AND PARTY?

DID YOU TAKE A GIFT?

WHO WERE THE GODPARENTS?

PHOTOGRAPH

THE EARLY YEARS

How often did you see them when they were young? Did you see them regularly?

....

....

....

....

....

....

....

....

....

....

....

....

....

....

....

....

....

....

....

What was their name for you? What do they call you now?

....

....

....

....

....

....

....

....

....

....

Did you have pet names for them?

....

....

....

....

....

....

....

....

DID THEY INVENT ANY OF THEIR OWN WORDS FOR THINGS WHEN THEY STARTED TALKING?

WHAT'S THE FUNNIEST QUESTION THEY HAVE ASKED YOU?

WHAT OTHER THINGS DID THEY SAY OR DO THAT MADE YOU LAUGH OR SURPRISED YOU?

A Watchful Eye
VIGGO PEDERSEN (1854–1926)

THE EARLY YEARS

WHEN DID YOU FIRST SPEAK OR CHAT ON THE TELEPHONE? DO YOU REMEMBER ANY OF THEIR EARLY CALLS TO YOU?

....
....
....
....
....
....
....
....
....
....
....

....
....
....
....
....
....
....

HOW WAS THEIR GENERAL HEALTH DURING THEIR EARLY YEARS?

....
....
....

....
....
....
....
....
....
....
....
....
....
....
....
....
....
....

TAKING CARE
OF THEM

DID YOU BABY-SIT FOR THEM? DO YOU

REMEMBER THE FIRST TIME? ....

....

....

....

....

....

....

....

....

WHAT WAS THE LONGEST

TIME YOU LOOKED AFTER

THEM? WHEN WAS IT?

....

....

....

....

....

....

WHAT DID YOU MOST ENJOY ABOUT BEING

WITH THEM?

....

....

....

....

....

....

....

....

....

....

....

....

TAKING CARE
❧ OF THEM ❧

DID YOU FIND IT EASIER TO HAVE THEM ONE

AT A TIME OR TOGETHER? ....

....

....

....

....

....

....

....

....

....

....

....

....

....

....

....

....

....

....

....

....

WERE THERE SPECIAL THINGS THEY LIKED TO

DO AT BEDTIME? ....

....

....

....

....

....

....

....

DID YOU READ STORIES

TOGETHER? OR LISTEN

TO MUSIC? ....

....

....

....

....

....

....

....

....

Woman and Child Reading
KATE ELISABETH OLVER (D.1960)

DID THE WHOLE FAMILY EVER COME TO STAY TOGETHER? WAS THERE A SPACE PROBLEM WHEN THEY DID?

WHEN DID YOUR GRANDCHILDREN FIRST COME AND STAY BY THEMSELVES?

DID THEY COME OFTEN?

DID THEY EVER WAKE UP DURING THE NIGHT?

WHAT USUALLY HAPPENED IF THEY DID?

DID THEY EVER MISBEHAVE? WHAT DID YOU

DO?

DID HAVING THEM STAY FEEL VERY DIFFERENT

FROM WHEN YOUR OWN CHILDREN WERE

YOUNG?

WHAT WERE THEIR FAVOURITE FOODS? DID

THESE CHANGE OVER TIME? ....

....

....

....

....

....

....

....

....

WAS THERE ANYTHING THEY

REALLY DIDN'T LIKE TO EAT?

....

....

....

....

....

....

....

....

....

WHAT WERE THEIR FAVOURITE

GAMES? ....

....

....

....

....

....

....

WERE THERE ANY OF YOUR CHILDREN'S

GAMES OR TOYS THEY ENJOYED PLAYING

WITH? ....

....

....

....

....

....

....

....

....

....

Shelling Peas
WILLIAM BANKS FORTESCUE (D. 1924)

FAVOURITE THINGS

What sort of things did they enjoy doing with you?

....
....
....
....
....
....
....
....

Were there any jobs they particularly liked to help you with? (Cooking? Gardening?)

....
....
....
....
....
....
....
....
....
....
....
....
....
....
....
....
....
....
....

HOBBIES AND ADVENTURES

WHAT DID THEY MOST ENJOY DOING? DID
THEY HAVE ANY PARTICULAR HOBBIES?

....

....

....

....

....

....

....

....

....

....

....

....

....

....

....

....

WHAT 'CRAZES' DID THEY GO THROUGH?

....

....

....

....

....

....

....

....

DO YOU REMEMBER ANY CRAZES FROM YOUR
OWN CHILDHOOD?

....

....

....

....

....

....

....

....

....

....

....

....

HOBBIES AND ADVENTURES

WERE THEY PARTICULARLY TALENTED? WHAT
SEEMED TO COME MOST NATURALLY TO THEM?

DID THEY SHARE ANY OF YOUR OWN
INTERESTS?

HOBBIES AND ADVENTURES

DID THEY DO ANYTHING ADVENTUROUS OR

EXCITING? ....

....

....

....

....

....

....

....

WHAT WERE THE MOST SURPRISING THINGS

THEY DID? ....

....

....

....

....

....

....

....

....

....

DID YOU GO ON ANY

OUTINGS TOGETHER?

WHERE DID YOU GO,

AND WHEN? ....

....

....

....

....

....

....

....

....

....

....

....

....

....

....

....

....

....

....

CHRISTMAS

Did you usually spend Christmas together as a family? Was it usually on Christmas Day or another day?

....
....
....
....
....
....
....
....
....
....
....
....
....
....
....
....
....
....
....

Is there a particular Christmas you remember? What made it special?

....
....
....
....
....
....
....
....
....
....
....
....
....
....
....
....
....
....
....
....
....

The Christmas Tree
Elizabeth Stanhope Forbes (1859-1912)

CHRISTMAS

WHAT WERE THE BEST THINGS ABOUT
CHRISTMAS FOR YOU AND YOUR FAMILY? DID
YOU HAVE A TREE? DID YOU OPEN YOUR
PRESENTS TOGETHER?

WHAT SPECIAL CHRISTMAS MEMORIES OF
YOUR GRANDCHILDREN DO YOU HAVE?

HAVE THEY GIVEN YOU ANY PRESENTS YOU
PARTICULARLY TREASURE?

BIRTHDAYS

HAVE YOU BEEN TO ANY OF THEIR BIRTHDAY

PARTIES? ....

....

....

....

....

....

....

....

....

....

....

....

WHAT ARE THE MOST

SUCCESSFUL BIRTHDAY

PRESENTS YOU HAVE GIVEN

THEM? ....

....

....

....

....

....

....

HAVE THEY EVER CELEBRATED YOUR BIRTHDAY

WITH YOU? ....

....

....

....

....

....

....

....

....

....

....

....

BIRTHDAYS

WHAT BIRTHDAY PRESENTS HAVE THEY GIVEN YOU – DRAWINGS, PAINTINGS, CARDS OR LETTERS, FOR EXAMPLE? HAVE YOU KEPT ANY OF THEM?

PASTE A CARD OR
LETTER HERE

OTHER CELEBRATIONS

WHAT SPECIAL FAMILY CELEBRATIONS OR ANNIVERSARIES HAVE YOUR GRANDCHILDREN BEEN AT? WHO ELSE WAS THERE?

....

....

....

....

....

....

....

....

....

....

....

....

....

....

....

....

....

....

ARE THERE ANY FUTURE OCCASIONS YOU ARE PARTICULARLY LOOKING FORWARD TO?

....

....

....

....

....

....

....

....

....

....

....

....

....

....

....

....

....

....

OTHER CELEBRATIONS

HAVE YOU BEEN TOGETHER WHEN AN IMPORTANT NATIONAL OR INTERNATIONAL EVENT HAS OCCURRED? WHAT WAS IT?

DO YOU REMEMBER ANY SPECIAL GATHERINGS WHEN YOU WERE A CHILD?

PHOTOGRAPH

La Ronde des Enfants
GASTON DE LA TOUCHE (1854–1913)

HOLIDAYS

HOLIDAYS WE HAVE SPENT TOGETHER

DATE	WHO CAME	WHERE WE WENT	HOW LONG

HOLIDAYS

WHAT DO YOU REMEMBER ABOUT THE FIRST

HOLIDAY YOU WENT ON TOGETHER?

....
....
....
....
....
....
....
....
....
....
....
....
....
....
....
....
....
....
....
....

WHERE DID YOU STAY?

HOW DID YOU SPEND THE

TIME?

....
....
....
....
....
....
....
....
....
....
....

HOLIDAY
PHOTOGRAPH

HOLIDAYS

Did any of their friends ever come on holiday with you?

Where else would you like to go to together on holiday and why?

Where do you think they would enjoy going to on their own?

Going for a Paddle
EMILE CAGNIART (1851–1911)

PRIMARY

SCHOOL

WHEN AND WHERE DID THEY FIRST GO TO
SCHOOL?

DID YOU ATTEND ANY SCHOOL EVENTS?
(NATIVITY PLAYS? SPORTS DAYS?)

DID THEY EVER WIN A PRIZE?

PRIMARY SCHOOL

WHAT DID THEY MOST ENJOY
AT PRIMARY SCHOOL?

WHAT DID THEY SAY THEY WANTED TO DO
WHEN THEY GREW UP?

DID YOU SEE ANY OF THEIR SCHOOL
REPORTS?

SECONDARY SCHOOL

WHAT ABOUT SECONDARY SCHOOL DID THEY MOST ENJOY? (ACADEMIC WORK? SPORT? MUSIC? DRAMA? ART?)

....

....

....

....

....

....

....

....

....

....

....

....

....

....

....

....

....

WHAT IMPORTANT EXAMS DID THEY SIT? HOW DID THEY DO IN THEM?

....

....

....

....

....

....

....

....

....

....

DID THEY EVER WIN ANY PRIZES OR AWARDS?

....

....

....

....

....

....

....

....

SECONDARY SCHOOL

WHAT SCHOOL TRIPS OR HOLIDAYS DID THEY
GO ON?

DID YOU GET TO KNOW ANY OF THEIR
FRIENDS?

DID THEY KNOW WHAT THEY WANTED TO DO
WHEN THEY LEFT SCHOOL?

OVER
THE YEARS...

How have their characters developed
and changed over the years?

Do you recall the first proper
conversations you had together?

PHOTOGRAPH

OVER
THE YEARS...

WHAT DO YOU THINK ARE THE FINEST

QUALITIES OF EACH OF YOUR

GRANDCHILDREN? ....

....

....

....

....

....

....

....

....

WHAT DO YOU HOPE WILL BE IMPORTANT TO

THEM AS ADULTS? ....

....

....

....

....

....

....

DO PEOPLE SAY THEY ARE LIKE YOU IN ANY

WAY? ....

....

....

....

....

....

....

....

....

....

OVER
THE YEARS...

WHAT HAVE BEEN THE MOST EXCITING THINGS YOU'VE DONE TOGETHER?

....
....
....
....
....
....
....
....
....
....
....
....
....
....
....
....
....
....
....
....

WHAT SINGLE EVENT WITH EACH OF THEM HAS GIVEN YOU THE MOST HAPPINESS?

....
....
....
....
....
....
....
....
....
....
....
....
....
....
....
....
....
....
....
....

Happy Children
PAUL BARTHEL (1862-1933)

THE
FUTURE...

WHAT WOULD YOU MOST LIKE TO DO OR

SHARE WITH EACH OF YOUR GRANDCHILDREN,

AND WHY?

WHAT DO YOU HOPE THEY WILL BEST

REMEMBER YOU FOR?

THE
FUTURE...

WHAT ARE YOUR HOPES FOR THE FUTURE, FOR EACH OF THEM?

WHAT SINGLE PIECE OF ADVICE WOULD YOU OFFER EACH OF THEM, IF THEY ASKED YOU?

REFLECTIONS

WHAT HAVE BEEN THE MOST REWARDING
ASPECTS OF YOUR RELATIONSHIP WITH THEM?

....
....
....
....
....
....
....
....
....
....
....
....
....
....
....
....
....
....

DO YOU THINK THERE'S A SECRET TO HAVING
A HAPPY AND LOVING RELATIONSHIP WITH
GRANDCHILDREN?

....
....
....
....
....
....
....
....
....
....
....
....
....
....
....
....
....

Lazy Days
WILLIAM MARSHALL BROWN (1863–1936)

REFLECTIONS

ARE THERE ANY LITTLE MISTAKES YOU THINK YOU HAVE MADE AS A GRANDPARENT?

....
....
....
....
....
....
....
....
....
....
....
....
....
....
....
....
....
....
....
....
....

WHAT SINGLE THING ABOUT BEING A GRANDPARENT HAS GIVEN YOU THE GREATEST HAPPINESS?

....
....
....
....
....
....
....
....
....
....
....
....
....
....
....
....
....
....
....
....
....

Other illustrated record books available from Four Seasons Publishing include:

A Grandparents Book: The Story of our Life ISBN 1 85645 142 9
Mother's Journal: A Book of Memories ISBN 1 85645 150 X
Our Baby ISBN 1 85645 143 7
The Story of our Family in the Twentieth Century ISBN 1 85645 139 9